Devotion in Motion

Devotion in Motion

Joan Hake Robie

STARBURST company
LANCASTER, PA

First Printing (April 1981)

ISBN: 0-914984-00-4
Library of Congress Catalog Card Number 80-83298
Printed in the United States of America

To you
who delight to worship Him
with
body, soul, and spirit

Contents

Acknowledgements

The Camerons, for *The Dancing Heart;*

Tom and Roberta Corle, for cover design and book illustrations;

Suzanne Dussinger, model for cover illustration;

Glenn Eshelman Studio, photographer for cover illustration;

Marjorie Holmes, for *Dance of Worship;*

Sondra Lenore Jonson, for *Come Praise Him Evermore;*

The music publishers, whose credits appear below their songs.

COME PRAISE HIM EVERMORE

Dance! Let your thoughts
fly through the air!
Dance through adversities
singing, "I do not care!"
Be a downright Rebel when
life will chant, "No!"
Be stubborn within,
for with Jesus you glow.
Down the halls of your heart
let this message ring;
"I and my Saviour
can do anything!"

Sondra Lenore Jonson

DANCE OF WORSHIP

Lord, for those of us who love dancing, let us dance sometimes in prayer.

The spirit often physically reaches out toward you. The heart is filled with emotions that words can't always express. The mind teems with problems that often block the path to you.

Lord, as I move to this music I offer up all my feelings. My joy in this beautiful world, my awe and gratitude. My hopes and my dreams.

I offer you too in this dance my doubts and disappointments. My anxieties and grievances. I banish them, I break their chains. I cast them into the music and my body frees my spirit to dance before you as well.

Accept this dance as an act of worship, oh God, and draw near.

And now as I dance I would offer up all the people I should be praying for. As I lift my arms in adoration I gather them in for your blessing.

I see them happy. I see them well. This vision is vivid before me. As I dance I rejoice for their health, their happiness, their peace. These things I claim in your name for them.

I dance for the people I love, oh Lord. I dance their cares into your keeping.

But I also dance for myself. I dance in worship, to reach you.

Marjorie Holmes

THE DANCING HEART

David danced before the Lord
He danced with all his might;
His heart was filled with Holy joy,
His Spirit was so light.
Michal thru the window looked
To criticize his start,
She didn't know that David
Had got a dancing heart.

Chorus:

The Holy Ghost Will Get Your Feet A'Dancing,
The Holy Ghost Will Fill You Through And Through;
The Holy Ghost Will Get Your Feet A'Dancing,
And Set Your Heart A'Dancing, Too.

1
Believe It Or Not

BUDDHISTS use a "prayer wheel" and various body "motions" in their worship.

HINDUS make religious pilgrimages by repeated prostrations of the body on the ground. Rising up, and then down, mile after mile, they travel on. Their "motion" is geared to self-abasement.

AFRICAN tribes dance wildly in worship of their heathen gods — "motion."

MOSLEMS, as they pray, kneel and bend over until their heads touch the ground — "motion."

PSEUDO RELIGIONS of today, such as *Yoga,* with its *lotus position,* and ***Transcendental Meditation,*** in which worshipers *meditate* for hours on end as they take on various body positions, are "motion."

JUDAISM has kept "motion" alive throughout the centuries with its Hebrew dances.

CHRISTIANITY is the only religion in which "motion" *has not* been an integral part of its worship.

"Motion is dancing!" quips the born-again, fundamental, Bible-believing, Spirit-filled Christian. "That's worldly! It goes along with liquor, cigarettes, scantily-clad women, immorality, adultry. When I gave my heart to Christ I turned away from such things."

Others raise their eyebrows and complain, "With so much worldliness infiltrating the church of Jesus Christ we must guard against this sort of emotionalism and radical behavior."

Yet there are those who meet the challenge with, "It's been too long that the unGodly have dominated this form of expression. It's time for God's people to have freedom of worship, not only in the Spirit, but physically. After all, don't sport fans scream and yell when their team gets a home run or scores a touchdown? Why should the devil have total control of dancing? He's had it too long! It's time God's people began to dance!

THE DANCING HEART

David danced before the Lord
To magnify His Name,
In God's almighty Presence
He felt no sense of shame;
The oil of gladness flowed that day,
It quickened every part,
He hadn't only dancing feet,
He had a dancing heart.

Chorus:

The Holy Ghost Will Get Your Feet A'Dancing,
The Holy Ghost Will Fill You Through And Through;
The Holy Ghost Will Get Your Feet A'Dancing,
And Set Your Heart A'Dancing, Too.

2
From The Beginning

From the very beginning of man's existence, and throughout all civilizations, he has used dance to express joy, sorrow, hope, pain, and victory. Primitive people's religion was a major part of their life and religious dances were considered indispensible to expressing their religious beliefs. A great part of this dancing was group dancing, in which patterns with gestures brought out a theme or plan of action, such as a war dance. This creative expression could well have been the first art forms.

In 1415, in England, a great celebration was held to herald the return of Henry V after his victory at Agincourt. This celebration was adorned by maidens dancing with tambourines in their hands.

Martin Luther, a great man in religious history loved children and wrote many carols about them. He loved the free spirited little ones who went gleefully about, singing, skipping and dancing. Luther believed in that which was real and encouraged others to give all to God in total participation.

William Tyndale, a sixteenth century English church leader wholeheartedly believed the Scriptures and was not afraid to use a language of joy and gladness. In his Prologue to the New Testament he wrote, *"Euagelio (that we cal gosepl) is a greke word, and signyfyth good, mery, glad and ioyfull tydings, that maketh a mannes hert glad, and maketh hym synge, daunce, and leepe for ioye."*

The Roman Catholic Counter-Reformation, represented by the Council of Trent (1545-63) was determined to remove much literature and drama from the church. At Lyons, in 1566, the site of the synod meeting, priests and others were threatened with excommunication if they led dances in churches or cemeteries. The church tried desperately to stop religious dancing, but was not totally successful in doing it.

A defense of religious dancing was written in 1588 by Thoinot Arbeau. He says: *"For one who has spoken ill of dances, there are an infinity of others who have praised and esteemed them. The holy and royal prophet David danced before the ark of the Lord. And as for the holy prophet Moses, he was not angered to witness dancing, but grieved because it was performed round a golden calf, which was idolatry."*

Throughout Bible days, a great part of the worship of God was in dances performed by the children of Israel. When they crossed through the Red Sea and were delivered from Egyptian bondage, Miriam, the prophetess, led them in a song of triumph, during which time she *took a timbrel in her hand; and all the women went out after her with timbrels and with dances.* (Exodus 15:20)

II Samuel 6:14 says, *And David danced before the Lord with all his might.* He was so happy and he expressed this happiness by dancing. In the dance he, by the rhythmic motions of his body, showed the love and devotion he had for the Lord. His devotion was "in motion."

In I Samuel 18:6 we read, *it came to pass . . . when David was returned from the slaughter of the Philistine, that the women came out of all cities of Israel, singing and dancing, to meet King Saul, with tabrets, with joy, and with instruments of music.* (Tabrets are tambourines.)

The New Testament does not refer to religious dance, but, as you have read, there are references to the early church's use of the dance as an accepted expression of joy. In Matt. 11:17 Jesus said, *We have piped unto you, and ye have not danced;* indicating that he recognized the dance as a normal expression of joy, sorrow and other human situations. And, again, in the story about the rejoicing over the return of the prodigal son, the Lord mentions that there was dancing. Today we hear so much about physical fitness. Just take a short drive in your car on almost any day, rain or shine, and you are sure to see at least one, or more panting and sweating figures making their way along the road, oblivious to the traffic, rarely even stopping at city corners to look for oncoming vehicles.

Worship services of the early church were vastly different from those of today. Pulpits and pews were non-existent at this time. The first sermon preached from a lectern was done so that the congregation could hear their pastor who had a weak voice. It was not until the Reformation period that pews were introduced into the church. In an effort to give equality to all, the people were allowed to sit throughout the service as did the bishop. In most of our churches today the pastor stands above the people, on a platform, and behind a massive pulpit desk.

Were you to have walked into an early worship service you would have viewed a room set with just a few benches along the wall. This was to accommodate the elderly and the ill. Everyone else was expected to stand throughout the service, except during the times when it was necessary to kneel or prostrate themselves on the floor. The pastor would be found standing in the midst of the people as he read from the Scripture. When it was time for the sermon the people would sit down. Prayers of confession were usually done with the congregation prostrating themselves on the floor. At times they would kneel. During the prayers of praise and thanksgiving they would stand with arms raised. In Paul's letter to Timothy he said, *I will therefore that men pray everywhere, lifting up holy hands.* (I Tim. 2:8) Paul respected the body as a channel for religious expression.

From the sixth to the twelfth century the church became more authoritarian and started to regulate all forms of liturgical worship. Some of the dances were forbidden in the church. During this period cultural expression was at a standstill. The Mass developed at this time in which Gregorian chants accompanied sacred dance. It was customary to celebrate festivals and saints' days and processionals with some form of dancing. Relics of martyrs and saints were carried through the streets during these festivals. While there were efforts to do away with degenerate forms of dancing, sacred dancing spread throughout Europe during the 8th and 9th centuries. A painting by Cosmas, an Alexandrian monk, envisions the idea of the universe with the sun, moon and stars encircling the earth, and also reveals rhythmic patterns in the circling positions of the angels who held the stars and the two angels inside the circle who carried the sun and moon around the earth.

True worship comes from the heart, and the position of the body in worship only aids that heartfelt expression. You can worship the Lord with movement when you are sitting or standing, or even when you are lying down. This expression in worship can also be a time when you relax and breathe deeply, surrendering your whole self-body, soul and spirit to God. The Lord's Prayer lends itself to this form of worship and is a prayer which has universal interest and acceptance (see page 54). This could be a new beginning for you as you enter into this new but old mode of worship.

It is interesting to learn of the origins of the dances during the medieval period. To *carol* means to dance, and when you look at a hymnal you see that the hymns are separated into *stanza* and *chorus.* You are undoubtedly familiar with those two words but do you know what they mean? Their origins? *Stanza* means to stand or halt and *chorus* means to dance. Thus it was meant for the people to dance during the chorus and stop dancing during the stanza. There might have been a young man or woman do a solo dance during the stanza of a certain hymn. During the chorus the people did the *tripudium* step or better known, the *three step.* You take three steps forward and one back, three steps forward and one back, and so forth. Any 4/4 or 2/4 hymn can be sung or played with the tripudium, which means jubilation.

The tripudium step was danced with the people standing with many abreast, arms linked together in row after row. They danced out of the church and into the streets, then back into the church and then out into the streets again for the recessional. This three steps forward and one back is symbolic of the *moving ahead* of the believer.

However, it hasn't always been a move ahead. There were those who felt there was a need to "crucify the flesh" in repentance of their sins by physical abuse. In the eleventh century the Flagellants appeared in Northern Italy, and spread to Germany and later to Spain and England. Priests carrying crosses and banners led processions of people of all ages and classes. They walked, double-file, through the streets, reciting prayers and whipping themselves and others to draw blood from their bodies in supposed hope of repentance of their sins. Although this sort of thing was outlawed they have reappeared through the centuries in various countries throughout the world.

THE DANCING HEART

Out of Egypt long ago
The Israelites were led,
By a mighty miracle
They were all kept and fed;
Thru the Red Sea they were brought,
The waters stood apart,
And God gave Sister Miriam
A dance down in her heart.

Chorus:

The Holy Ghost Will Get Your Feet A'Dancing,
The Holy Ghost Will Fill You Through And Through;
The Holy Ghost Will Get Your Feet A'Dancing,
And Set Your Heart A'Dancing, Too.

3
There Was Motion

By the end of the early medieval period in history the church's rising hierarchy frowned on dancing with the congregation. Since dancing symbolized equality no longer did the priesthood desire to dance with the ordinary people. On days which were given for dancing worship priests would dance only with fellow priests and deacons would dance only with fellow deacons. The people would dance only with others of the congregation, not with deacons nor with priests. Just as today, there are those who would deviate from the norm. So it was in that day. Certain priests, undoubtedly those who were more self-confident and did not feel threatened by the members of the congregation, joined in the people's dancing. This brought great disapproval from the other priests and soon the rising hierarchy encouraged church legislation against all dancing. When dancing in the church was forbidden it went outside the church by way of funerals. Since the church hierarchy felt threatened by the equality of the dance in the church they forbade participation in it. The graveyard dance, or funeral dancing represented the future equality of all people — priest, or church hierarchy and com-

mon people alike.

Before the legislation against dancing a dance group known as the Chorizantes sprang up in Germany. Absorbed in fantastic visions, they would, as though in a trance, go dancing through the street and in and out of churches, continuing with their dancing until they fell with exhaustion. In 1419 this type of dancing occurred at Strasbourg. Tradition had it that St. Vitus had cured the emperor's son of demonic possession. Thus, the ecstatic dancers put on their display invoking St. Vitus, who had been martyred in the third century, to cure a malady. Gradually the name St. Vitus became connected with nervous diseases, and chorea. Thus the name, St. Vitus dance.

In Fire dances, the most ancient of the "Christianized" pagan dances, persons leaped over or through fires. It was believed that the flames and smoke had properties for health, in that the flames and smoke supposedly destroyed miasma and vemin.

Health was a very sought after condition during the medieval period. During a period of fifty years, the Black Plague wiped out half the population of western Europe. A funeral song was introduced at this time called *Ring Around the Rosie*. Does this song sound familiar to you? Perhaps you, like me, played a childhood "circle" game while you sang this song. *Ring around the Rosie, a pocket full of posies, Ashes,*

ashes, we all fall down. Did you know that this is an English funeral song? Here is what it means: *Ring around the Rosie* — Rosie was the pock marks on the cheeks of those who had contracted the disease of the Black Plague. *A Pocket Full of Posies* — those who have died from the Plague. *Ashes, ashes* — also denotes the dying or funeral of those cut down by the Plague. The English version of "Ashes, ashes" was

"Ahchew, ahchew." which meant sneezing, one of the signs
that a person was getting the Plague. *We all fall down* − we
are all going to die. This song was sung not as a sorrowful
song, but a song of hope and joy for the coming Kingdom of
God. The suffering of this life is bearable when we think of
the glory to come.

During the later medieval period emotional expression and
drama were popular. Although the church had denounced
secular theatrical productions, it created its own dramatic
portrayals by introducing more choral songs, picturesque
processionals, and ceremonial dances. This, the church hoped,
would draw more interest in its services. During the twelfth
and thirteenth centuries monks used to dance and pray for
the salvation of the universe. Franciscan monks sang and
danced and called themselves the singing servants of Christ.
Fourteenth century hymn writers made numerous references
to ring dances and processional dances. In the fourteenth
century a German monk composed several hymns which the
choristers sang during the performance of their three-step and
ring dances.

The fourteenth to the seventeenth centuries saw dances for
curing disease. Most were performed in the honor of the
apostle John, Saint Anthony, or the Virgin Mary. The dance
seemed to bring people some relief from pain. What was
known as "dance carols" were widely known during the
medieval and Renaissance periods. The *Dance of Death* was
the most popular dance of that era. It was known as *Dance
Macabre* and was danced in Spain, France, England and Germany. Dominicans and Franciscans preached sermons on the

terrors of death, thus convicting sinners to repentance.

In the seventeen hundreds the term "choir" was understood as an elevated and enclosed area of the church where symbolic movements were often performed.

The end of the Renaissance period (1700) seriously threatened creative expression within the church — both Roman Catholic and Protestant. Neither would allow sacred dances in their service. Finally, it was the Reformation with its fight against church tradition — images, pilgrimages and the worship of saints, that did away, almost entirely, with church dances. Arts of sculpture, drama, and painting, along with dance, were totally taboo in the Protestant church. The Puritans even called these forms of expression the *sport of the devil.* But the Puritans did have movement in their worship, more than most other churches had. When they prayed they stood with their arms raised above their heads as was done during the time of the early church. Through diligent study of the Bible they learned that this was the common Biblical way to pray.

There was great emphasis on seriousness of the mind in worship. The opinion was that the spirit could be entered through the mind rather than through the senses. In spite of this thought there were those like John Cotton, a New England Puritan, who did not totally condemn this form of worship. He wrote, "Dancing I would not simply condemn, for I see two sorts of mixt dancing in use with God's people in the Old Testament; the one religious (Exodus 15:20-21), the other civil, tending to the praise of conquerors (I Sam. 18:6-7)." Another Puritan, Increase Mather, condemned only

dancing which aroused the passions. But, it can be safely con-
cluded that the close of the 17th century brought a near end
to religious dancing. At this time in history it was generally
accepted that religious dancing was the work of pagan in-
fluence in the church. The 18th century religious dance was
scarce and scattered and the 19th century revealed few signs
of a revival. It seemed that religious dancing was gone forever;
however this form of expression in worship though now sup-
pressed was to be resumed many years later.

THE DANCING HEART

There was a celebration
Upon the Red Sea shore,
Timbrels rang, desert sand
Became a dancing floor;
The people sang and praised God there,
He made the gloom depart;
And put to dance, the love and joy,
So deep down in their hearts.

Chorus:

The Holy Ghost Will Get Your Feet A'Dancing,
The Holy Ghost Will Fill You Through And Through;
The Holy Ghost Will Get Your Feet A'Dancing,
And Set Your Heart A'Dancing, Too.

4
When The Spirit Moved

Camp meeting time during the 19th century did include methods of worship which may have indicated a trend back toward religious dance. As the worshipers met they welcomed one another by the shaking of hands. Then they would be seated with women sitting in rows on one side of the room and the men on the other side, all facing forward. Men and women were separated only by an aisle, with slaves behind the minister's platform during most of the service. During the service there would be dancing and other movements such as "jerking" when the Spirit touched the worshipers. When it came time to march out of the service all barriers would be torn down and black and white folks alike would join in for this marching song. This would end the service for that day. Since the worship during these camp meetings tended to equalize worshipers it presented a threat to black suppression. The Southern legislatures did not like the sense of freedom which this form of worship granted slaves.

The Shakers were a religious group which was founded in England. A small representation of Shakers came as colonists to New York in 1747. They grew considerably after the Revolution and by 1850 their number increased to 6,000 followers. In the worship of Shakers rows of benches would be set up for the beginning of the service. When it was time for dancing to begin these benches would be pushed against the walls. Those who did not wish to join in the dance worship would simply sit on the benches along the walls. Disillusioned with formal worship Shakers used dance as a means to their expression. They created intricate religious dances. The name Shaker came from the rapid movement of their hands with most of the action in the wrists. When the participants shook their hands with the palms turned down toward the floor, the symbolic motion meant that they were shaking out "all that is carnal." When the palms were turned upward as if to receive spiritual blessing, the quick up and down shaking movement expressed the open petition, "Come life eternal." Aside from this common motion of the hands, there were many pantomimic gestures to interpret their songs. General movements included bowing, bending, and a great deal of turning. This movement symbolized turning away from evil and around toward good. The key step which the Shakers did was the *square order shuffle.* Many different patterns were used in this dance. Basically, it was "two sets forward and one set back, then one set forward." (A set is four steps of: right foot forward striking the heel and then ball of the foot, then left foot forward striking the heel and then the ball of the foot, then the right foot forward in the same manner.) Circling dances were very popular during this time. Ezekiel's *Wheel in the middle of the wheel* (Ezekiel 1:16). Patterns like moving square, double square, cross and diamond, square and

compass and finished cross, were all popular forms of dance. The *continuous ring* in the shape of a C moving into serpentine style was a pattern which the Shakers loved. They believed that we should use the whole body — the hands, the feet, the tongue, to express the inward reverence of the soul.

A sacred order called *The Free and Accepted Masons,* was organized in 1717. This secret society evolved out of an English guild of masons who were building English cathedrals. The moral code of the masons was based on the symbols of the *level,* the *compass,* and the *plumb.* God was thought to be the *Great Architect* of the *Universe.* Masons conducted elaborate rituals in their initiation ceremonies and the bestowing of degrees. Their members sat around the edge of the hall, leaving the center for special marches and the formation of floor patterns of specific designs. These formations gave each member a feeling of belonging and a common bond. To this day the bond among the members of the order is, for some members, greater than that of the church. Just read the obituary column of a local newspaper account of a departed member of the Masons. You will read that a special funeral ceremony was held by the order for the departed Mason.

By the end of the 19th century worship with movement was unaccepted in the established churches. Protestant missionaries made it clear to their converts that the Christianity they presented had no place for movements for the worshiper. The only accepted form of movement was to bow the head or to kneel. South Africans referred to a *Christian* as *"he who has given up dancing."* In spite of this, some missionaries, however, effectively adapted native religious dances to the worship of God.

THE DANCING HEART

The Prodigal was far away
Wand'ring out in sin,
But he came back to father's house
And father took him in;
He put a robe upon his son,
The merriment did start,
The Prodigal got dancing shoes
To match his dancing heart.

Chorus:

The Holy Ghost Will Get Your Feet A'Dancing,
The Holy Ghost Will Fill You Through And Through;
The Holy Ghost Will Get Your Feet A'Dancing,
And Set Your Heart A'Dancing, Too.

5
It's Not For Me

Only a few religious dances have remained into the 20th century. The wedding dance, traditional throughout Europe, is still used in the Greek Orthodox churches of today. Those who participate in the *ring dance,* which is performed around the altar at the conclusion of the ceremony, are the priest, the bridegroom, the bride, and the koumbaro. The koumbaro is the man or woman who stands up for the wedding. They must be of Orthodox faith. The priest takes the groom's hand, the groom takes the bride's hand, and the bride takes the hand of the koumbaro. Then, as the priest leads, they all dance joyfully around the altar three times. The three times around the altar signifies the Father, Son, and Holy Spirit.

But the Greek Orthodox are not the only ones who kept dance in the church alive. The negroes (blacks) helped keep motion alive throughout the years, and into this century. Movement has always been a part of their worship. Clapping, swaying, foot stomping — yes, the dance has always characterized their worship.

In America and abroad both Catholic and High Episcopal

services have used symbolic movement. Did you know that
the Catholic mass contains symbolic movement — kneeling,
standing, sitting, then standing, sitting and kneeling again —
motion?

Today, Catholics and Protestants alike are coming together
in Christian love and concern for the "body of Christ." One
result of this unity in the love of Christ is singing and dancing
— whether spontaneous, in the Spirit, or a choreographed
dance choir. Symbolic movement, perhaps portraying a Biblical theme, has been added to the liturgical services of some
mainline denominations. Sometimes, as the congregation sings,
solo dancers are used to interpret the stanzas of the hymns.

In I Corinthians 6:19-20 Paul speaks of our bodies as temples of the Holy Ghost and that we should glorify God in our bodies as well as in our spirits. Verse 19 says, *What? know ye not that your body is the temple of the Holy Ghost which is in you, which ye have of God, and ye are not your own?* Verse 20: *For ye are bought with a price: therefore glorify God in your body, and in your spirit, which are God's.* These Scriptures can have many applications — glorify God in your body by not over indulging in eating and drinking, sexual activity, in what you hear and see — television, movies and more. Jim Bakker of the television program, PTL Club, said recently, on one of his television programs, "God put rhythm, singing, and dance within us to worship Him. It's a high form of worship and is being brought back into the church. On the day of Pentecost there was dancing, and also when the paralytic was healed there was dancing. The paralytic 'leaped'."

To be sure, when you attempt to get a congregation into worship in motion there are those who will feel shy about participating, or they might not want to take part at all. They are really saying that they want to see others participate before they will try it. There are always those who are not willing to try something new until they see it performed. Let them participate in the singing.

Little children will be the first ones to want to join the activity. They are eager for action and will enthusiastically join in the dance. This is something they can do even if they cannot understand the sermon. The psychology of it is that worshiping the Lord is good and if I may use the word "fun." After all, our Lord had a sense of humor. Jesus knew that it would be more difficult to get adults doing something new than it would be for children. That, I believe, is why he said, *Unless you turn and become like one of these, you shall not enter into the kingdom.*

In order to get adults into it you should begin with an "easy motion" song; one which does not require too much physical movement. Then, as they feel comfortable with this you can move on to more involved symbolic expressions. Something like *The Lord's Prayer* is a good beginning. Most anyone would not object to the movement accompanying this song. It is entirely, or for the most part, hand and arm movement. As you feel comfortable with this you can move on to other choruses with more movement:

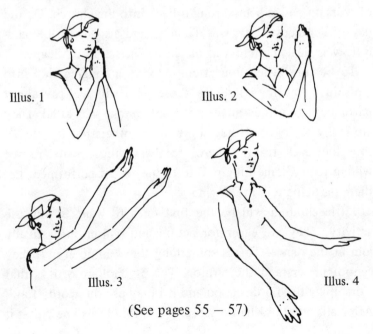

Illus. 1

Illus. 2

Illus. 3

Illus. 4

(See pages 55 – 57)

Our Father, Who art in heaven

Place hands together as in prayer; allowing your mind to be cleared of all distractions and cares of the day. Focus your whole being on God. (Illus. 1)

Hallowed be Thy Name,

Still keeping hands closed in prayer, raise them slowly upward. As you do this also raise your head upward as you look toward Heaven. (Illus. 2)

Thy kingdom come, Thy will be done.

Begin to open your hands and arms wide as you also open your soul to God and His vastness. (Breathe deeply as you do this.) (Illus. 3)

On earth as it is in heaven.

Head is lowered to look into the present or reality of this earth with its needs of the day. Palms are turned downward. This is our willingness to do God's will upon this earth where we live. (Illus. 4)

Give us this day

Hands again are clasped in submission as in Illus. 1.

Our daily bread;

Reaching out to God in supplication for our daily needs, but at the same time resting in His loving care. (Illus. 2)

And forgive us our debts

Total yieldedness to the forgiveness of our Lord means opening ourselves to His cleansing stream. (Illus. 3)

As we forgive our debtors.

We are forgiven our sins and likewise we forgive others without reservation. Our lowering of our arms signifies our reaching out to forgive others. As we do this we ask God's forgiveness and let him flow out of us. (Illus. 4)

And lead us not into temptation

Again our hands are clasped together in supplication and
prayer for guidance and help in the time of temptation. We
must be yielded to the Holy Spirit with a oneness and single-
ness of purpose so that we not enter into sin. We are not fear-
ful, but confident of His love and care for us. (Illus. 1)

But deliver us from evil

We again reach up to God, knowing that without Him we
cannot resist the evil forces of this universe. Our upstretched
hands signify our childlike dependence upon the power of
God's deliverance. (Illus. 2)

For thine is the kingdom, and the power, and the glory

Our hands open to signify God's vast dominion. By opening
our arms we open ourselves up to His power and glory and we
are overwhelmed by His love. We praise and worship Him in
the beauty of His holiness. (Illus. 3)

forever. Amen.

With hands again turned downward we return our thoughts again to the needs of man upon this earth. We want God's Holy Spirit to forever dwell within us and through us and use us to minister to those about us. And with the word, AMEN we pray, "And so be it." (Illus. 4)

If you are planning a service with symbolic movement you can let the people know in advance (after they have had an introduction to it), and have everyone move into the auditorium or sanctuary in a *procession-like* manner. Be sure you direct them to fill the front pews. This way you will have them all together and thus more united. However, before you have them go to the pews you might want to lead them down one aisle and up another, and possibly around the inside of the church. They will most likely feel more comfortable if you have them sing as they walk, with hymnbook in hand. When there is a real festive occasion you might like to have the congregation proceed outside and around the church singing. This will not only be inspiring to your congregation, but also draw onlookers who might decide that this church is rather "interesting," "neat," "contemporary" or whatever — a church they'd like to attend. The medieval church and some of the New England churches used to proceed into their worship services in this manner. Can you believe that King David danced up and down the streets when he brought the ark of the Lord into Jerusalem? Can you visualize the Old Testament prophets playing the drums, trumpets and tambourines and shouting praises to God in a worship service? There is nothing which compares to a communion service at dawn on the desert — if you happen to live near a desert. Perhaps you live near a beach. Celebrate with an Easter sunrise service on the beach. Have a soloist sing *Rise Again* by Dallas Holmes. Another time you might invite a Jewish believer to lead in the dance, *hora.* Praise God, this dance will

bring to your rememberance the days that our Lord walked this earth. I wouldn't be surprised that he participated in dancing his native dances. For Jesus was not only the Son of God, He was a man who walked this earth. What could be more earthly than being a carpenter? So, if He was a carpenter and did such earthly thing like build houses I am sure that He participated in dancing his native dances, as well as Jewish celebrations. Didn't He say, *We have piped unto you, and ye have not danced.* (Matt. 11:17) I recall an outdoor candle-light service I went to in a church in southern California. It was held on Christmas Eve and was so impressive and inspiring — all the candles lit in the darkness as we processed into a circle for the next part of the festivity.

THE DANCING HEART

The father's house with music rang
To welcome home his son,
Wine was flowing, full of glee
All misery was gone;
The elder brother looking on,
Complained it wasn't fair,
He hadn't got a dancing heart
But we hope he joined them there.

Chorus:

The Holy Ghost Will Get Your Feet A'Dancing,
The Holy Ghost Will Fill You Through And Through;
The Holy Ghost Will Get Your Feet A'Dancing,
And Set Your Heart A'Dancing, Too.

6
Let The Children Dance

Dramatic movement is one form of worship which children enjoy because it gives them an opportunity to express what they think, see and feel. It is a learning and sharing experience in which they can respond with their own ideas and in their own way. The development of this creative expression will lead to a fuller, richer life. Church education leaders are coming to realize that learning is more meaningful to children if they are involved in creative, dramatic movement. Symbolic movement can be used while singing hymns or carols or even while praying. When using symbolic movement with children, as well as adults, it might be best not to refer to it as "dance." One reason is that symbolic movement might then be considered as too difficult, or in some circles sinful or worldly. Neither should it be called "rhythms" because that term is often used for activities of younger children — like "rhythm bands."

Christian education should seek the development of the whole person — body, soul and spirit. Children need rhythmic movement to direct the energies of their active, growing bodies. Directing these energies into worship goes a long way toward reaching the goal of development of the whole person.

Symbolic movement is an art form which is used to express and interpret ideas, insights and moods. It is a natural expression which can be individual or collective. It can be simple body movement which flows freely with feeling, or it can be a more complex arrangement of expression which communicates inner thoughts and patterns which are carefully planned but allow for the communication of inner feelings. These patterns may be repeated to form a complete whole. First, the individual or group decides what they wish to convey, whether a spontaneous message or the enactment of Bible drama such as The Good Samaritan. You need to assign 'parts' like robbers, travelers and The Good Samaritan, and, of course, the traveler. Practice the parts before putting the story together. One child can play the part of the traveler who was robbed and beaten, others can play — the Levite — the priest, etc. Posture — body movements, can well describe this dramatic scene. This story is a great one to allow real freedom of expression — the anguish and hurting of the traveler — the lack of concern by the passers-by, and the deep compassion of The Good Samaritan. First you must get into postures which the various characters might have had and then various motions done with intensity will make the story come alive.

In the story of Daniel you can have a Daniel, lions, a prison guard, and even other characters of your own creation. Each actor can simulate his own particular character's walk, or, in the portrayal of the lions, getting down on all fours should bring forth "real" lions. Acting out Bible stories not only teaches children the story itself, but also drains off tension and hostilities through action.

Children need to get so involved with the stories that they will never forget them. — Thus the Bible comes alive. It is up to the leader or director to help get things started. Then let the child or children experiment creatively while the leader maintains firm control. He or she communicates by eye or words with each child, and encourages him to discuss verbally any new ideas he might have. The leader should allow plenty of time for the child to speak.

Group participation allows for the sharing of ideas, individual creative expression, and exploration. It is up to the leader to find and improve on weak areas, superficial areas, and meaningless areas. A child may not be able to aptly express himself verbally but, as is often the case with a creative child, he is able to communicate by dramatic movement better than he can communicate verbally. On the other hand, a highly verbal child may be overtalkative as vent for his insecurities. He may find it very difficult to express himself with dramatic movement.

Emotionally disturbed or retarded children find release from the natural expression of dramatic action.

Walking, clapping and singing are equally enjoyed by young and old alike. Songs like *This Little Light of Mine* and *His Banner Over Me Is Love* can be used effectively to give enjoyment to all. Children like to skip and turn, swing their arms, and clap vigorously.

You as a leader should be the example of what you want the children to do. Pictures of Biblical themes and written Scripture are great aids in explaining the story you wish to portray. Children like to imitate. They will see the way you act more than hear what you say. In other words, *actions speak louder than words.* Pretending can be fun. Dipping fingers into an imaginary bowl of paint, and painting a rainbow in space can create lots of action and fun. Make wide curves reaching high in the sky and then down to earth. Each child should try to see what they discover in the rainbow. This can bring out many new ideas and concepts. The children will get great joy out of this movement.

We've all heard the spiritual folk song "Dry Bones." (Ezekiel 37:1-10) The song speaks of the various bones of the body and how they are attached to each other — from head to toe. In order for the body to function properly there must be proper movement of each part of the body. Movement is essential to the health of the body. Exercise is vital. President Kennedy saw the importance of a healthy nation — a healthy people. That is why he instituted so many physical fitness programs — jogging, etc. God desires that we take care of our bodies and not hurt them.

In I Corinthians 12:14-31 Paul speaks of the church as a body having many parts, but all related to one another. Therefore, if one part of the body suffers, they all suffer. So it is important that every member of the church body as well as every part of our own individual bodies be kept healthy. Essential to the development of a child is growth, and exercise is essential to growth. If you don't believe it just watch a baby kick in the crib or a two year-old trying to get free of the restraining hold of his mother. We know that if we want to keep children interested in a Vacation Bible School or church or Sunday school program we've got to have lots and lots of activity. Songs that they can move to — clap their hands, bend and stretch, feel free. As a young child grows older he wants more and more activity. That is why it takes church and Sunday school leaders who are well trained in guiding these active little bodies into worship which incorporates physical expression. Heads held high, spreading the arms wide, stretching the legs. Every child enjoys songs like "Bend and stretch, reach for the stars, Here comes Jupiter, there goes Mars, etc." Playing rhythm instruments is another "movement" expression for children and can make worship a fun experience. Children would rather run than walk. If you don't believe it just let a class of 7 and 8 year-olds loose on a playground. They don't walk to the swing — they run to the swing. Did you ever see a child prancing about or, rather, dancing about, while waiting for his or her mother to finish shopping? The more restless and tired they become, the more they dance about.

So, why not put this love of movement to work for God rather than the devil? Children love circle games like, *The Farmer In The Dell,* or *In And Out The Window,* where as the children make a circle, one child skips "in and out the window" under the arms of those in the circle, adding another child to the line as the song is repeated. Many of these "school playground" kind of action songs can be adopted to songs about the Lord and Christian life. Various moods can be expressed by the way a child or children walk — happiness, sadness, joy, fear, hope. The interpretation of parables is a great way to use symbolic movement. The Good Samaritan, the ten virgins — so many can be adapted for use with children.

The interpretation of Psalms like the 150th can incorporate the use of "instruments" as well as singers and dancers. Instruments can be made by the children themselves and you will be amazed at their creativity. — Never let the practice session become work — let the children offer suggestions and free their expression. After all, worship is the individual expression of one's love for the Lord, and it should always be free and spontaneous as is possible.

Praise the Lord, Praise the Lord with the sound of the trumpet:

It makes no difference what age a person is he can enjoy worship encouraged by Scripture. Practically every church has someone or two who play the trumpet. As worship with this Psalm begins the voice of the trumpets begin to rise. Praise the Lord, praise the Lord — perhaps you will want a vocal choir to sing this.

Praise the Lord, Praise the Lord with the lute and the harp:

If your congregation is fortunate enough to have a harpist, he or she can call forth the heavenly sounds. — A harp can be a beautiful expression of angelic sound. If you don't have a harp let the organist simulate the sounds of a harp.

Praise the Lord with the timbrel, the timbrel and the dance:

Here you might like to have young people take part. If your

church is one where more physical expression is accepted, you could have the young people with the timbrels and cymbals dance in skips and leaps.

Alleluia, Alleluia, Alleluia, Alleluia — Here you can have more group expression — perhaps swaying and turning freely as they face one another as they praise God with the Alleluias.

Another good song for children, at holiday time is *Deck The Halls:*

Deck the halls with boughs of holly:

Have the children, while standing in a line and holding Christmas wreaths high, dance to the left, with a light, springy step.

'Tis the season to be jolly:

Same movements as before, except move to the right.

Don we now our gay apparel:

While holding wreaths high turn in the place where you are standing.

Troll the ancient, yuletide carol:

Take 1st position again and move to the left.

Then, on the last *fa la la la la* move to the right, holding wreaths high in the air.

DECK THE HALLS

Let's just praise the Lord! The word of God says in I Timothy 2:8 *I would that men would pray everywhere, lifting up holy hands."* Hands, with palms up, reach up to seek or to receive; hands, with palms down, move with compassion or work with diligent skill. Hands reaching out, seek contact with others — extending beyond self-centeredness. Hands reveal the unseen tensions of each individual and they communicate response consciously and unconsciously. In Nehemiah 2:18 we read, *"So they strengthened their hands for this good work."* Hands lifted up can also indicate our surrender to the will of God.

(See pages 107 & 108)

THE DANCING HEART

Now saints are cold and bound
By unbelief today,
They want the blessing of the Lord
But worry what men say;
O, let the Lord have full control
From dead traditions part,
And He will set you free within,
You'll have a dancing heart.

Chorus:

The Holy Ghost Will Get Your Feet A'Dancing,
The Holy Ghost Will Fill You Through And Through;
The Holy Ghost Will Get Your Feet A'Dancing,
And Set Your Heart A'Dancing, Too.

7
Stir Up The Saints

THERAPY

Although there are those of us who dare to believe in the power of God to instantly deliver those who are in emotional or physical bondage there are occasions when expert medical help is the necessary route to take. After all wasn't Luke a physician? Songs with simple movements are therapeutic to those with emotional illnesses. I recall some years ago when I was doing substitute teaching. This one particular school had students who were emotionally handicapped. Getting through to these children was no easy task. In fact, just having a substitute teacher could cause them to lose control. (They might become ill and throw up or become hysterical.) They become so dependent on their regular teacher — so used to his or her personality and method of communication that any change becomes an emotional crisis. You might encounter desks turned over — objects thrown around the room. On one occasion I was teaching music to young children of about six years old. One little brown-haired girl, with long braids and cute dimples in her cheeks, seemed to be unreachable. Her regular teacher had told me that she didn't respond to anything. — Just sat there — blah!

Well, through prayer and reaching out with all that was within me I found that music was the key to unlock the door to this sweet little girl's heart. I put on a record with a lively, catchy tune and began to dance about to the music. Her eyes lit up and with a little encouragement she was on her feet — dancing — responding to the communication of music. Praise God, I'd reached out to her through music and she took my hand. What a breakthrough! What a joy! The delivering power of the Holy Spirit can heal sick minds and emotions. Hallelujah!

A chorus with very easy motions is *Let Us Break Bread Together.* If you are able, get down on your knees. Place hands on either side of your face as if facing "the rising sun." (Illustrations below) Then, as you sing, *Oh Lord, have mercy on me,* while still on your knees, raise arms heavenward in supplication. This chorus also can be sung with motions, while in a sitting position, without getting down on your knees.

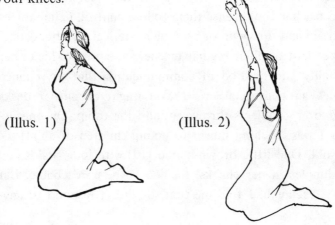

(Illus. 1)   (Illus. 2)

LET US BREAK BREAD TOGETHER

Unknown

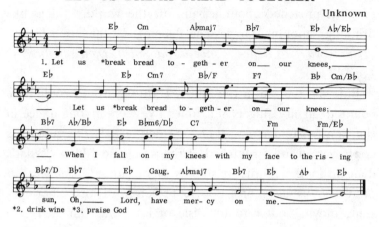

*2. drink wine *3. praise God

The physically handicapped — deaf, blind, etc., can likewise be led into a fuller expression of worship as they make use of the faculties they possess. Take Joni Eareckson — the now famous mouth artist, who, due to a diving accident some years ago is paralyzed from below her neck down. This talented young woman creates beautiful landscapes and figures through the use of a pen or brush held between her teeth. What a challenge to dedicated believers to commit themselves to helping the physically handicapped to a fuller, more useful life. Acceptance, encouragement and prayer are the keys to unlock doors for the handicapped.

Why for so many years have we used motion with children — in their songs and in drama? It unites them into one whole. Thus you as the leader can reach your goal of teaching them how to worship. Likewise motion has a therapeutical effect on adults, freeing them from many psychological hangups about themselves and their bodies.

As a child growing up in the World War II years I heard sermons preached about leaving off the worldly things like drinking, smoking, movies and dancing. Mother used to say, *"If you want to dance, dance in the Spirit. Dance before the Lord."*

But who danced in the Spirit? Until recently, I could have counted on my fingers the times I've seen anyone dance in the Spirit. I understand that for some readers this subject is controversial and far-fetched. Perhaps you are asking, "What's dancing in the Spirit? It sounds sacrilegious." *Dancing in the Spirit* usually consists of a person with his or her eyes shut, moving out into the aisle or into the altar area of a church. He or she will sway and move with the music as though in a trance. Most of the time this experience is spontaneous, and there is just one dancer at a time in a church service. Rarely, until the last few years, has more than one dancer participated in a given service. Today you might see two persons or more dancing joyfully around the altar and down the aisles, or possibly, the entire congregation dancing. This latter form of dancing is usually done with eyes open and with the person or persons not in a "trance-like" state. This is not to say, however, that they are not in the Spirit. The atmosphere in this kind of worship is permeated with the same power of God as is the atmosphere in the service where a person or persons dance in a "trance-like" state. Until recently, only a few churches encouraged either form of dance in their worship service. I remember an elderly lady from my home church. At times, during our *altar service* after the regular preaching service was over and the congregation as a whole was kneeling or sitting before the altar, this little lady of 89 or so pounds would "toe" dance in a small circle around the area at the altar. This was a precious sight to see, and reassuredly, this little lady's life backed up her expression of worship to the Lord. Ordinarily, she was a rather shy woman, never pushing herself to be seen of others. Other times I have seen her dance all around a church sanctuary, eyes closed, stepping around or over every obstacle and never bumping into anything or anyone.

The Bible speaks of "dancing," but it does not give instruction as to dancing as a practiced form of worship or dancing in an unpracticed form, or, as we call "in the Spirit." (Neither does the Bible speak of "singing" as a "practiced form" of worship.) Many Pentecostal people think of "in the Spirit" only as being in a "trance-like" state, but is this always the case?

In this day and age, especially among *charismatic* circles, a somewhat different style of dancing has developed. Just as a whole congregation is led in singing, so can a whole congregation be led in dancing or movement. Rhythmic songs of praise, hope and victory lend themselves to sacred dancing. With eyes open, whole congregations can worship joyously with their bodies. If you have ever been in a service where they had a *Jericho March* you would understand better how delightful and exhilarating this united worship can be. Here again, I remember when I was a child . . . during a time of praise and rejoicing, our church body would, spontaneously, or at the suggestion of the pastor, form a line around the walls of the sanctuary. Then, to the tune of a song like, *The*

New Jerusalem, we would march around the church singing,
"They'll be singing, they'll be shouting, when the saints go
marching home — to Jerusalem — to Jerusalem. Waving palms
(and at this point we would raise a handkerchief high as a
banner) with loud 'hosannas' as the saints go marching home
to the new Jer-u-sa-lem." There were other songs too, in
which we clapped hands as we walked. Could it be that such
outward expressions like this would have a therapeutical effect on worshipers today which might result in fewer nervous
breakdowns among the saints of God?

Both practiced dancing and "in the Spirit" dancing can be
equally effective in our worship of God. One is no more
"holy" than the other, nor is one sacrilegious and not the
other. Since true worship comes from within, it doesn't matter what outward form it takes so long as it is not offensive
or unbecoming to a Christian and can be substantiated by the
Scriptures. Both methods of dancing for the Lord, or unto
the Lord bring glory and honor to Him.

However, when we are worshiping God in a certain way, if
we are charitable towards God's people, we won't run rough-
shod over their traditional convictions or offend them. Paul
said in 1 Corin. 6:12: *All things are lawful unto me, but all
things are not expedient!* Instead, we "excel to the edifying
of the church." The Holy Spirit is always courteous and dis-
creet. And *the spirits of prophets are subject to the prophets.*
(1 Corin. 14:32) Michal, daughter of Saul, observed David worshiping God in a dance. She despised him and criticized him,
and a curse came upon her. (2 Sam. 6:23) We should be cau-
tious about analyzing and finding fault with sincere Christians

who are worshiping God or doing works of God. Perhaps some people reason that *in the Spirit* dancing, or *in a trance* dancing means one is totally under the control of the Holy Spirit, and therefore cannot be determined as dancing *in the flesh.* Could it be that this is excusing or relieving oneself of any responsibility in the matter?

Be encouraged, dear Christian friend, and don't feel guilty because you have a yen for physical expression. This in itself is not sinful. When that physical expression is coupled with a desire for worship and is based on love for Christ it becomes a beautiful form of worship. *The parts which do not look beautiful have a deeper beauty in the work they do, while the parts which look beautiful may not be at all essential to life! But God has harmonized the whole body by giving importance of function to the parts which lack apparent importance, that the body should work together as a whole with all the members in sympathetic relationship with one another.* I Corinthians 12:23, 24, 25 (Phillips translation)

THE DANCING HEART

In the Bible we can read
That in the latter days,
Men would leave their first love
And turn to carnal ways;
But true ones turn to Jesus
For the Bridegroom set apart,
Awaiting for His coming
With a joyful, dancing heart.

Chorus:

The Holy Ghost Will Get Your Feet A'Dancing,
The Holy Ghost Will Fill You Through And Through;
The Holy Ghost Will Get Your Feet A'Dancing,
And Set Your Heart A'Dancing, Too.

8
Let's Celebrate

BANNERS

Banners are a way of saying, "This is a **Celebration!**" We celebrate Christ and what he has done for us. The young and the young-in-heart will enjoy having a part in making banners. If your church has a sewing circle ask the ladies to help. They will delight at turning their creativity into praise to the Lord. They can look through their sewing baskets for buttons, beads, sequins, braid, ric-rac, etc. to be used to beautify the banners. Felt, patchwork, velvet, velour, and burlap are all great fabrics from which you can make the banners. Even paper can be used to create something beautiful for the Lord. There are unlimited variations you can use. Let each one draw a design on paper first, then from there they can begin with the fabrics. Scripture verses burst forth with life as they are magnified on banners. The beautitudes become meaningful as they are displayed with bright colors.

My father-in-law, a perky fellow of 89 years, who pastors a little white frame country church, remarked to a much younger city pastor, "You are having revival meetings? Where are the banners? People walking by your church will never know you are having revival meetings if you don't make your services inviting." Perhaps banners, are not your "cup of tea," but this old gent knows, after over 40 years of evangelistic ministry and the remainder as a pastor, that if you want people to come into your meeting you've got to advertise. That's the name of the game. "Banners — outside and in —" says my father-in-law, "will let folks know something is about to happen. There's life at that church!" *Beautify the house of the Lord.* (Ezra 7:27) So, start now — let the world know that **"Jesus Lives!"**

HAND CLAPPING

A great way to express devotion in motion is Hand Clapping. We read of it in Psalms 98:8 *Let the floods clap their hands: let the hills be joyful together.* Also in II Kings 11:12 *And he brought forth the king's son, and put the crown upon him, and gave him the testimony; and they made him king, and anointed him; and they clapped their hands, and said, God save the king.*

Clapping is not always done as approval, for in Lamentations 2:15 we read *All that pass by clap their hands at thee; they hiss and wag their head at the daughter of Jerusalem, saying, Is this the city that men called The perfection of beauty, The joy of the whole earth?* Clapping for the saints has a manifold purpose. Someone has said that clapping is a powerful weapon of the children of God. Clapping can be done in unison, agreeing together that: (1) All satanic powers are bound and have to leave; (2) We beckon the angels of the Lord to come to meet our needs; (3) The anointing of the Holy Spirit comes upon us and we are cut free from all earthly anxieties and cares; (4) Clapping as a body is powerful and we are pulling down the strongholds that the enemy, satan would set up before us.

As we clap before the Lord and unto the Lord we begin to rise up, as it were, with unity of strength and praise to the Lord. It is a dynamic expression and tends to lift you up into the heavenlies. As you clap, begin to send up prayer requests to the Lord as the Holy Spirit brings various needs before you. As you do this it is as though each need ascends to the throne of grace where the Lord is waiting to meet that need.

Have someone read **Psalms 98** as your prayer group begins
to clap:

1. *O sing unto the Lord a new song; for he hath done
marvellous things: his right hand, and his holy arm, hath
gotten him the victory.*

2. *The Lord hath made known his salvation: his righteousness hath he openly shewed in the sight of the heathen.*

3. *He hath remembered his mercy and his truth toward
the house of Israel: all the ends of the earth have seen the
salvation of our God.*

4. *Make a joyful noise unto the Lord, all the earth: make
a loud noise, and rejoice, and sing praise.*

5. *Sing unto the Lord with the harp; with the harp, and
the voice of a psalm.*

6. *With the trumpets and sound of cornet make a joyful
noise before the Lord, the King.*

7. *Let the sea roar, and the fulness thereof; the world, and
they that dwell therein.*

8. *Let the floods clap their hands: let the hills be joyful
together*

9. *Before the Lord; for he cometh to judge the earth: with
righteousness shall he judge the world, and the people with
equity.*

Another Psalm to clap is: **Psalms 150**

1. *Praise ye the Lord, Praise God in his sanctuary: praise him in the firmament of his power.*

2. *Praise him for his mighty acts: praise him according to his excellent greatness.*

3. *Praise him with the sound of the trumpet: praise him with the psaltery and harp.*

4. *Praise him with the timbrel and dance: praise him with stringed instruments and organs.*

5. *Praise him upon the loud cymbals: praise him upon the high sounding cymbals.*

6. *Let every thing that hath breath praise the Lord. Praise ye the Lord.*

Psalms 47 and **Psalms 8** are also good to use with clapping.

THE OFFERING

In Malachi 3:10 the scriptures tell us to *Bring ye all the tithes into the storehouse, that there may be meat in mine house, and prove me now herewith, saith the Lord of hosts, if I will not open you the windows of heaven, and pour you out a blessing, that there shall not be room enough to receive it.*

The offering can be a beautiful time of giving of our tithes and offerings and also of ourselves. Have those who wish to come forward to place their offerings in the plates. They could remain there in the front of the church and form a concentric circle around the altar. Songs or choruses of praise and worship can be sung, ending with the doxology. As they sing the doxology those in the circles can join hands, face into the circle, and as they sing words to the doxology, *"Praise God from whom all blessings flow"* take four steps forward into the circle while raising up each others' hands above their heads. When they come to *"Praise Him all creatures here below,"* take four steps backwards and bow from the waist as they lower hands to their sides. *"Praise Him above ye heavenly host."* (Same as in 1st phrase.) *"Praise Father, Son, and Holy Ghost"* — do the same as in the second phrase. On the *"Amen"* all hands still joined are raised above heads.

LIVING SCULPTURES

During a church family night you might wish to develop a series of "living sculptures." People should separate in groups of about five. Each group is then asked to prepare movements interpreting a certain portion of a given Scripture or the words of a hymn or chorus. For example, *The Lord's Prayer* could again be used here. The first group could interpret *Our Father who art in heaven, Hallowed be Thy Name.* (Then this group "freezes" in position.) The second group would interpret *Thy Kingdom come, Thy will be done on earth as it is in heaven.* (This group freezes in position.) The third group: *Give us this day our daily bread. And forgive us our debts as we forgive our debtors.* (Then freeze.) The fourth group: *And lead us not into temptation, but deliver us from evil.* (Then they freeze.) The fifth group: *For thine is the kingdom, and the power, and the glory forever. A-men.* Fifth group freezes as they finish the A-men. Run through the entire presentation again and again until the symbolic movements become easier to do. And it does get easier as individuals begin to forget themselves and their bodies and get lost in worship and praise to our Lord.

Another excellent portion of Scripture would be Genesis 22 where we read of Abraham's call from God to sacrifice his son Isaac. Here we would not form groups but as individuals: take positions which express how Abraham must have felt when he was called to sacrifice his son. Then, the second time through, the group could take positions which express how Isaac must have felt when he realized what his father was planning to do to him. The third time through the group takes positions signifying Abraham and Isaac's delight when God announced that Isaac was to be spared. A fourth time through take positions which picture Abraham's joy when he looked up and saw the ram in the thicket (which would mean that he would not have to sacrifice his son after all). God had provided a sacrifice.

If "living sculptures" is too ambitious for you try doing *The Lord's Prayer* in this way:

All stand in a line with hands crossed and joined to one another:

Our Father, Who art in heaven

Unfold arms very slowly as you continue with:

Hallowed be Thy Name,
Thy kingdom come, Thy will be done.

On earth as it is in heaven.

All cup hands as you say:

Give us this day our daily bread;

Bend over in submission with:

And forgive us our debts
As we forgive our debtors.

Take hands again (crossed, as before), slowly bend heads as you pray:

And lead us not into temptation, but deliver us from evil

Uncross arms slowly and raise heavenward in adoration and praise as you say:

For thine is the kingdom, and the power, and the glory Forever. Amen.

Amazing Grace

AMAZING GRACE

John Newton

(Illustrations on page 103)

Amazing grace!

How sweet the sound

Touch lips on the word "sweet." (Illus. 1)

that saved a wretch like me!

Cross arms, touching the shoulders, as if in self-condemnation — head should then bow. (Illus. 2)

AMAZING GRACE — cont.'d

I once was lost,

Cup one hand over corner of one eye, as looking for someone. (Illus. 3)

but now am found,

Take hand away from forehead.

was blind,

Eyes closed, fingers touching the center of the closed lids.
(Illus. 4)

but now I see.

Move fingers from eyes and cup around eyes as if looking at
something. (Illus. 5)

*Praise God, Praise God, Praise God, Praise God, Praise God,
Praise God, Praise God.*

Arms high above head move from left to right and repeat
until the seventh Praise God at which time you move arms to
the middle position. (Illus. 6 - 7 - 8)

Repeat *Praise God* as before. (seven times)
Same motions as before. (Illus. 6 - 7 - 8)

AMAZING GRACE – cont.'d

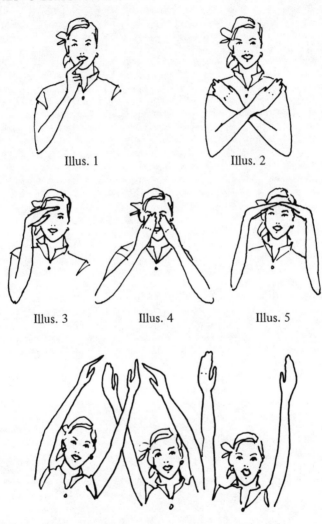

Illus. 1   Illus. 2

Illus. 3   Illus. 4   Illus. 5

Illus. 6, 7, 8

Thy
Loving Kindness

THY LOVING KINDNESS

Unknown

1. Thy lov - ing kind - ness
2. I lift my hands up

1. Thy lov - ing kind - ness is bet-ter than
2. I lift my hands up un - to Thy

is bet-ter than life, Thy lov - ing
un - to Thy name I lift my

life, Thy lov - ing kind - ness
name, I lift my hands up

kind - ness is bet-ter than life;
hands up un - to Thy name;

is bet - ter than life;
un - to Thy name;

My lips shall

THY LOVING KINDNESS — cont.'d

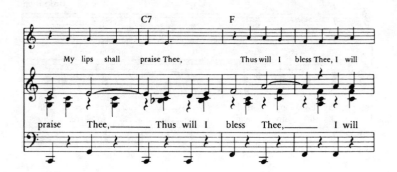

My lips shall praise Thee, Thus will I bless Thee, I will
praise Thee,_____ Thus will I bless Thee,_____ I will

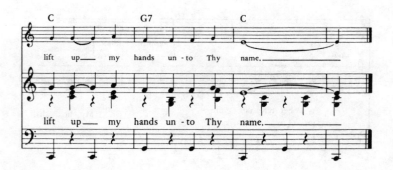

lift up___ my hands un-to Thy name.
lift up___ my hands un-to Thy name._____

Let's Just
Praise The Lord

LET'S JUST PRAISE THE LORD

William J. & Gloria Gaither

*voice
*hands

Spirit Of
The Living God

SPIRIT OF THE LIVING GOD

Daniel Iverson

Spir - it of the liv - ing God, fall fresh on me; Spir - it of the liv - ing God, fall fresh on me. Break me! Melt me! Mold me! Fill me! Spir - it of the liv - ing God, fall fresh on me.

(Illustrations on pages 116 & 117)

Spirit of the living God,

Hands raised heavenward. (Illus. 1)

fall fresh on me;

Move hands as though sprinkles of rain are falling. (Illus. 2)
(Repeat above)

Break me!

To break as with a hammer. Right hand pounds left hand. (Illus. 3)

SPIRIT OF THE LIVING GOD – cont.'d

Melt me!

Smooth out hands, from crossed position and separate them. (Illus. 4 & 5)

Mold me!

"Mold" with two hands. (Illus. 6)

Fill me!

To fill, as with a cup. Two hands form a cup. (Illus. 7)

Repeat as above:

Spirit of the living God, (Illus. 1)
fall fresh on me. (Illus. 2)

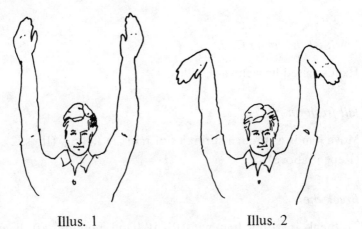

Illus. 1   Illus. 2

SPIRIT OF THE LIVING GOD — cont.'d

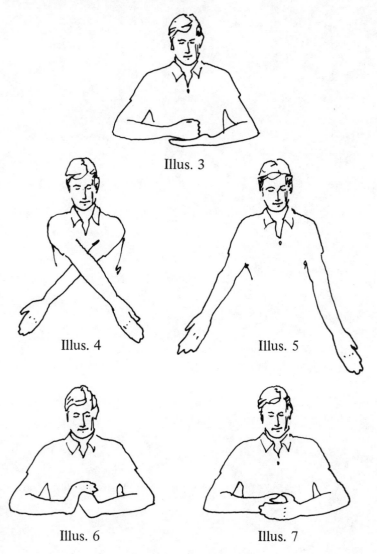

Illus. 3

Illus. 4   Illus. 5

Illus. 6   Illus. 7

Reach Out
And
Touch The Lord

REACH OUT AND TOUCH THE LORD

Bill Harmon

Reach__ out and touch the Lord____ as He__ walks by. You'll find He's not too bus-y to hear your cry. He's pass-ing by this mo-ment your needs to sup-ply. Reach out and touch the Lord____ as He walks by.

(Be creative with this one. Make up your own motions.)

Fill My Cup, Lord

FILL MY CUP, LORD

Richard Blanchard

1. Like the wom-an at the well I was seek-ing_____ For things that could not sat-is-fy. And then I heard my Sav-ior speak-ing:___ "Draw from my well that nev-er shall run dry."
2. There are mil-lions in this world who are crav-ing_____ The pleas-ure earth-ly things af-ford. But none can match the won-drous treas-ure_____ That I find in Je-sus Christ, my Lord.
3. So, my broth-er, if the things this world gave you_____ Leave hun-gers that won't pass a-way. My bless-ed Lord will come and save you_____ If you kneel to Him and hum-bly pray.

CHORUS

Fill my cup, Lord,___ I lift it up, Lord.___ Come and quench this

FILL MY CUP, LORD – cont.'d

thirst-ing of my soul.   Bread of heav-en, feed me till I

want   no   more; Fill my cup, fill it up and make me whole.

His Banner
Over Me
Is Love

HIS BANNER OVER ME IS LOVE

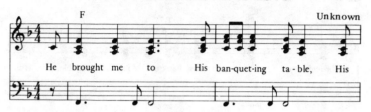

He brought me to His ban-quet-ing ta - ble, His

ban-ner o -ver me is love. He

brought me to His ban-quet-ing ta - ble, His

ban-ner o -ver me is love. He

HIS BANNER OVER ME IS LOVE — cont.'d

(Illustrations on pages 131 – 134)

Note: Where the phrase "He brought me to His banqueting table" is used, the following and other verses may be added:

2. "I'm my Beloved's and He is mine"
3. "He lifted me up into heavenly places"
4. "Jesus is the Rock of my Salvation"
5. "He is the Vine; we are the branches"

HIS BANNER OVER ME IS LOVE — cont.'d

(Illustrations on pages 133 & 134)

Verse 1

He brought me to His banqueting table,

Raise right hand heavenward for "He brought me to His" (Illus. 1)

Spread hands from center outward for "banqueting table." (Illus. 2)

His banner

Place hand over head to indicate "banner." (Illus. 3)

over me

Point to self with right hand. (Illus. 4)

is love.

Indicate "self" by crossing arms across "heart" area of chest. (Illus. 5)

(Repeat verse 1 two times, then end with "His banner . . . ")

Verse 2

I'm my Beloved's and He is mine,

Indicate "closeness" by crossing arms across heart area of chest. (Illus. 6)

His banner over me is love.

Motions as above. (Illus. 3 - 4 - 5)

(Repeat verse 2 two times, then end with "His banner . . . ")

HIS BANNER OVER ME IS LOVE — cont.'d

Verse 3

He lifted me up into heavenly places,
With palms turned upward, raise hands up in several positions.
(Illus. 7)

His banner over me is love.
Motions as before. (Illus. 3 - 4 - 5)
(Repeat verse 3 two times, then end with "His banner . . . ")

Verse 4

Jesus is the Rock of my Salvation,
Indicate "rock" by pounding fists together. (Illus. 8)

His banner over me is love.
Motions as before. (Illus. 3 - 4 - 5)
(Repeat verse 4 two times, then end with "His banner . . . ")

Verse 5

He is the Vine;
Raise arms from "waist level" upward to "above height"
position to indicate growth. (Illus. 9)

we are the branches.
With arms still held high, turn palms out and downward to
indicate "branches." (Illus. 10)

His banner over me is love.
Motions as before. (Illus. 3 - 4 - 5)
(Repeat verse 5 two times, then end with "His banner . . . ")

HIS BANNER OVER ME IS LOVE — cont.'d

Illus. 1

Illus. 2

Illus. 6

Illus. 3

Illus. 4

Illus. 5

HIS BANNER OVER ME IS LOVE — cont.'d

Illus. 7   Illus. 8

Illus. 9   Illus. 10

They'll Know
We Are Christians
By Our Love

THEY'LL KNOW WE ARE CHRISTIANS BY OUR LOVE

Words and Music by Peter Scholtes

1. We are one in the Spir-it, We are one in the Lord, We are one in the Spir-it, We are one in the Lord, And we pray that all u-ni-ty may one day be re-stored.
2. We will walk with each oth-er, We will walk hand in hand, We will walk with each oth-er, We will walk hand in hand, And to-geth-er we'll spread the news that God is in our land.
3. We will work with each oth-er, We will work side by side, We will work with each oth-er, We will work side by side, And we'll guard each man's dig-ni-ty and save each man's pride.
4. All praise to the Fa-ther, From whom all things come, And all praise to Christ Je-sus, His on-ly Son, And all praise to the Spir-it, who makes us one.

Chorus

And they'll know we are Chris-tians by our love, by our love, Yes, they'll know we are Chris-tians by our love. (by our love.)

THEY'LL KNOW WE ARE CHRISTIANS BY OUR LOVE — cont.'d
(Illustrations on page 140)

(Illustrations on page 140)

Verse 1

We are one in the Spirit,

Group holding hands move to the right. (Illus. 1)

We are one in the Lord.

Group moves to the left. (Illus. 2)
(Repeat above.)

And we pray that all unity may one day be restored.

Drop hands and stand in position.

Chorus:

And they'll know we are Christians by our love, by our love.
Yes, they'll know we are Christians by our love.

Embrace the person on your right, then the one on your left.
(Illus. 3)

Verse 2

We will work with each other,
We will work side by side.

Group in circle as before pretends as though the are working.
(Illus. 4)
(Repeat above two sentences.)

THEY'LL KNOW WE ARE CHRISTIANS BY OUR LOVE – cont.'d

And we'll guard each man's dignity and save each man's pride.

Drop hands and stand in position.

Chorus:

Repeat as before. (Illus. 3)

Verse 3

All praise to the Father,
From whom all things come,
And all praise to Christ Jesus,
His only Son,
And all praise to the Spirit,
who makes us one.

Hands are raised heavenward throughout this whole verse. (Illus. 5)

Chorus:

Repeat as before. (Illus. 3)

THEY'LL KNOW WE ARE CHRISTIANS BY OUR LOVE – cont.'d

Illus. 3

Illus. 1

Illus. 4

Illus. 5

Illus. 2

When The Saints
Go Marching In

WHEN THE SAINTS GO MARCHING IN

1. Oh, when the saints _____ go march-ing in,
2. And when the rev - e - la - tion comes,
3. And when they crown _____ Him King of Kings,
4. And when the sun _____ no more will shine,
5. And on that hal - le - lu - jah day,

1. Oh, when the saints go march - ing in;
2. And when the rev - e - la - tion comes;
3. And when they crown Him King of Kings;
4. And when the sun no more will shine;
5. And on that hal - le - lu - jah day;

1. Lord, how I want to be in that num - ber,
2. Lord, how I want to be in that num - ber,
3. Lord, how I want to be in that num - ber,
4. Lord, how I want to be in that num - ber,
5. Lord, how I want to be in that num - ber,

1. When the saints go march - ing in.
2. When the rev - e - la - tion comes.
3. When they crown Him King of Kings.
4. When the sun no more will shine.
5. On that hal - le - lu - jah day.

WHEN THE SAINTS GO MARCHING IN – cont.'d

Oh, when the saints go marching in,

Group of people walking in file, in a "marching" fashion.
(Illus. 1)
(Repeat)

Lord, how I want to be in that number,

Move into a circle and then point as though counting. (Illus. 2)

When the saints go marching in.

Move back into file again. (Illus. 1)

And when they crown Him King of Kings,

Move again into a circle and pretend as though you are plac-
ing a crown on your head. (Illus. 3)
(Repeat)

Lord, how I want to be in that number,

(Illus. 2)

When they crown Him King of Kings.

(Illus. 3)

(Illustrations on page 145)

WHEN THE SAINTS GO MARCHING IN — cont.'d

Illus. 1

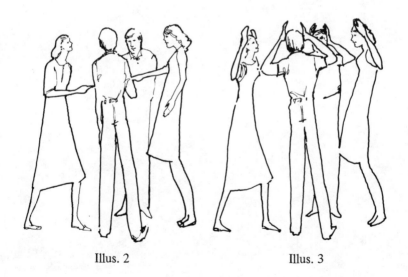

Illus. 2   Illus. 3

The 23rd Psalm

THE 23rd PSALM

The Lord is my shepherd;

Point upward with right hand index finger.

I shall not want.

Put arms around shoulders as if to cloak oneself in a garment.

He maketh me to lie down in green pastures:

Clasp hands together (outstretched) and place to left side of head. Bend head as if going to lie down.

he leadeth me beside the still waters.

Move outstretched fingers in ripple fashion to signify water.

He restoreth my soul:

Put hands flat across chest.

he leadeth me in paths of righteousness

Place hands parallel to one another as if to channel (guide) something.

for his name's sake.

Place right index finger on lips as if you are speaking the Lord's name.

THE 23rd PSALM — cont.'d

Yea, though I walk

Move feet as if walking.

through the valley of the shadow of death,

Move hands to symbolize mountains and valleys.

I will fear no evil:

Clench fists as you look heavenward. You are gaining strength and fortitude as you look to the Lord in the midst of evil around you.

for thou art with me;

Close eyes and move head slightly to and fro with firm assurance of the closeness of the Lord.

thy rod and thy staff, they comfort me.

Pretend as though you are picking up rod and staff with each hand. Then cross hands to top of shoulders as if to comfort.

Thou preparest a table before me in the presence of mine enemies:

Spread hands from center and separate as you "spread across the table."

thou annointest my head with oil;

With middle finger touch forehead.

THE 23rd **PSALM** — cont.'d

my cup runneth over.

Form a cup then, raising hands gracefully divide and lower them.

Surely goodness and mercy shall follow me

Raise hands for "surely goodness."
Raise hands higher in greater supplication for "and mercy."
Move one hand ahead of the other and vice versa to signify "shall follow me."

all the days of my life:

With one finger move as if counting.

and I will dwell in the house of the Lord for ever.

Raise hands as high as possible for "and I will dwell."
Form "house" with hands for the house of the Lord.
"For ever" — spread arms wide as possible.

(Illustrations on pages 152 — 154)

THE 23rd **PSALM** — cont.'d

I shall not want.

The Lord is my shepherd;

He maketh me to
lie down in green
pastures:

He restoreth my soul:

He leadeth me
beside the still waters.

he leadeth me in
paths of righteousness

THE 23rd PSALM — cont.'d

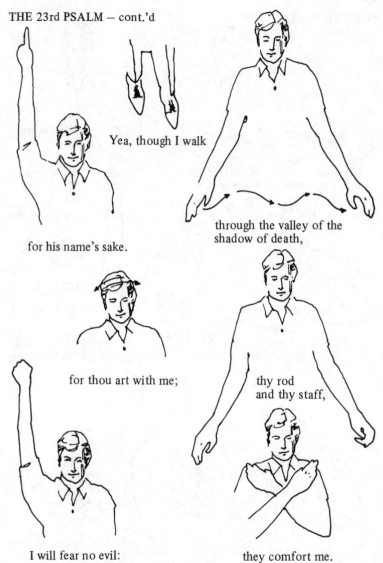

Yea, though I walk

for his name's sake.

through the valley of the
shadow of death,

for thou art with me;

thy rod
and thy staff,

I will fear no evil:

they comfort me.

THE 23rd PSALM — cont.'d

Thou preparest a table before me
in the presence of mine enemies:

thou annointest my
head with oil;

my cup runneth over.

Surely goodness and
mercy shall follow me

all the days of
my life:

and I will dwell in
the house of the Lord   for ever.

We are living in perilous times — economic crisis with its runaway inflation has resulted in the devaluation of the dollar and is threatening our very existence. People are rushing madly about to purchase gold and silver before prices soar beyond the reach of the average person. Food prices have risen to unbelievable heights. There exists a lack of patriotism, gross civil disobedience, and a breakdown in family structure. Growing tension in the Middle East as well as around the world prepares the way for World War III.

More than ever before, it is time that Christians forget their individual differences and stand together, loving and encouraging one another in the faith. A time of tribulation is coming upon the earth, tribulation such as the world has never known.

But praise God, he has given us the victory! Psalms 30:11 says, *"Thou hast turned for me my mourning into dancing: thou hast put off my sackcloth, and girded me with gladness.* We need to put our rejoicing into motion. To let God move our bodies as well as our spirits, for the body expresses that which is within the spirit.

The time has come for us to quit bemoaning our physical features and appreciate that body which is made in the likeness of God. Then, present body, soul, and spirit to Him in worship. For when we are able to surrender totally to the Lord it will be as a sweet smelling incense to our God. We then will find release in the outer as well as the inner man and our worship will become an experience of glorious freedom.

The book was not written solely to present the history of symbolic movement in worship, nor was it written only to provide songs of worship and the technique for incorporating worship into motion. It was written to encourage believers to set their body, soul, and spirit free to worship Him. In John 8:36 we read: *If the Son therefore shall make you free, ye shall be free indeed.* Who doesn't want to be free?

BIBLIOGRAPHY

Adams, Doug. *Involving The People In Dancing Worship • Historic and Contemporary Patterns.* Illinois: The Sacred Dance Guild 1975.

Soner, Pat. *Using Movement Creatively In Religious Education.* Boston: Unitarian Universalist Association 1963.

Taylor, Margaret Fisk. *A Time To Dance.* Illinois: The Sharing Company 1967.

Taylor, Margaret. *Dramatic Dance With Children In Education And Worship.* Illinois: The Sharing Company 1977.

Taylor, Margaret. *Look Up And Live.* Illinois: The Sharing Company 1953.

Zdenek, Marilee and Champion, Marge. *Catch The New Wind.* Texas: Word Incorporated 1972.